The Martian Museum of Earth Animals

An out-of-this-world adventure!

Written by
JULES HOWARD

BLOOMSBURY
CHILDREN'S BOOKS
LONDON OXFORD NEW YORK NEW DELHI SYDNEY

Illustrated by
MATT HUNT

DEAR MARTiANS,

AS HEADTEACHER OF THE SCHOOL, iT iS MY PLEASURE TO REMiND PARENTS THAT THE ANNUAL SLEEPOVER AT THE MARTiAN MUSEUM OF EARTH ANiMALS WiLL TAKE PLACE THiS EVENiNG. WE HOPE iT WiLL BE VERY EDUCATiONAL AND, AS ALWAYS, iNSPiRE LOTS OF DiSCUSSiON ABOUT THE iNCREDiBLE ANiMALS THAT LiVE ON OUR BEAUTiFUL NEiGHBOURiNG PLANET, EARTH.

PLEASE ENSURE YOUR CHiLD BRiNGS PYJAMAS, A SNOOZLE BAG AND A TORCH.

SOME PARENTS HAVE RAiSED CONCERNS ABOUT WHETHER THE CHiLDREN WiLL BE SAFE SPENDiNG THE WHOLE NiGHT iN A MUSEUM. TO THiS i SAY, PLEASE DO NOT WORRY. WE'VE DONE THiS TRiP MANY TiMES! NOTHiNG CAN GO WRONG.

SiNCERELY YOURS,

MYRTLE THE MANY-HEADED HEADTEACHER

BLOOMSBURY CHILDREN'S BOOKS
Bloomsbury Publishing Plc
50 Bedford Square, London, WC1B 3DP, UK
Bloomsbury Publishing Ireland Limited
29 Earlsfort Terrace, Dublin 2, D02 AY28, Ireland

BLOOMSBURY, BLOOMSBURY CHILDREN'S BOOKS and the Diana logo
are trademarks of Bloomsbury Publishing Plc

First published in Great Britain 2025 by Bloomsbury Publishing Plc

A catalogue record for this book is available from the British Library

ISBN: PB: 978-1-5266-6277-4;
eBook: 978-1-5266-7412-8

2 4 6 8 10 9 7 5 3 1

Printed and bound in China by
Toppan Leefung Printing, DongGuan, GuangDong

FSC
www.fsc.org
MIX
Paper | Supporting
responsible forestry
FSC® C104723

To find out more about our authors and books visit
www.bloomsbury.com and sign up for our newsletters
For product safety related questions contact
productsafety@bloomsbury.com

Lolo and Flarp were on a very exciting school sleepover at the Martian Museum of Earth Animals.

'Planet Earth is **AMAZING**,' said Flarp, snuggling into a sleep-pod. 'Even if the animals are a bit **WEIRD**.'

'Mostly it's a planet of beetles,' Lolo added. 'But if you look closer there's **SO MUCH ELSE** going on too!'

They had just started to drift off to sleep when suddenly there was a loud

CRASH!

IN ONE END ... OUT THE OTHER!

Most Earth animals are shaped like a tube, with a hole at one end where food goes in and a hole at the other end where poo comes out.

Welcome to the
Martian Museum of Earth Animals

Earth is full of animals!
In total, there are more than
two million different kinds!
Some **CREEP!** Some **CRAWL!**
Some **THRILL!** Some **KILL!**

*Come explore our galleries
to learn more!*

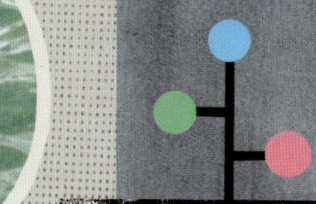

ARMOURED ANIMALS

Most Earth animals wear a suit of armour, known as an exoskeleton. Look carefully and you will see that a tiny minority (just 5 per cent) of animals have bones inside the body.

Invertebrates

This way for INTRIGUING INVERTEBRATES, INCREDIBLE INSECTS, FANTASTIC FISH, AMAZING AMPHIBIANS, REMARKABLE REPTILES, BRILLIANT BIRDS . . . and more!

→

Lolo and Flarp jumped out of their SKINS! Then they jumped out of their SNOOZLE BAGS and SLEEP-PODS.

'Has something broken in?' asked Lolo.

'Let's investigate!' said Flarp, who was always brave. 'THIS WAY!'

Straight ahead of them was a MASSIVE STICKY
SPIDER-WEB – with a huge hole in it.

'Look, Flarp,' said Lolo. 'I think whoever has
broken in CRASHED straight through that web.'

But Flarp wasn't listening.
He was gazing at the spiders.
'WOW, eight legs!' he said.
'That's so ... CUTE!'

Then they saw something **TRULY TERRIFYING** – a tall, lumpy, creature lurching towards the insect gallery.

INTRIGUING INVERTEBRATES!

Animals without backbones are called **INVERTEBRATES!**

Come and be wowed by **WONDERFUL WORMS!**
Be swept away by **SLIMY SNAILS!**
Be shocked by the secrets of **SPIDERS!**

↓

DRUMMING DELIGHTS

As well as making webs for catching flies, spiders also use their silky threads to communicate. This spider is tapping out a secret message to impress a nearby female.

WORLDWIDE WONDERS!

Invertebrate animals outnumber bony animals by more than a million-to-one. Other animals like to eat them. Without invertebrates, many animals would die out.

'A MONSTER!' cried Lolo.

Flarp was eager to keep moving. 'Come on, we've got to catch them! Let's follow this thread from the spider-web.'

They followed the thread LEFT and RiGHT and ROUND and ROUND...

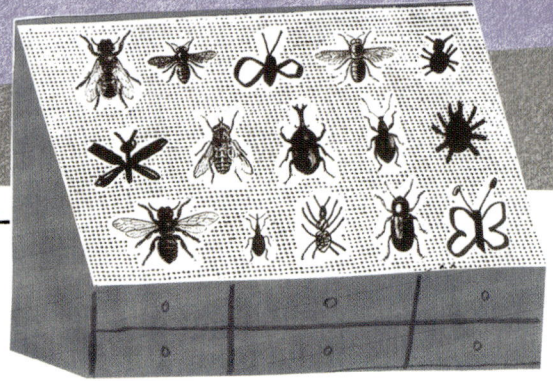

ROLL-UP, ROLL-UP!
By rolling dung up and burying it, dung beetles are nature's recyclers. A single beetle can roll a dungball 1,000 times its own weight. That's like a Martian picking up an asteroid!

INCREDIBLE INSECTS!

Did you know 90 per cent of all animals on Earth are insects?
See their SCISSOR JAWS! Meet their GHOULISH GAZE!

BUZZING ABOUT

Many Earth plants are sneaky! They make a special drink called nectar that insects get addicted to. When the insect slurps it up, they carry away pollen to other plants.

THE GIFT OF LIFT

This ant can lift in its jaws an object that is 5,000 times heavier than it. How much can you lift?

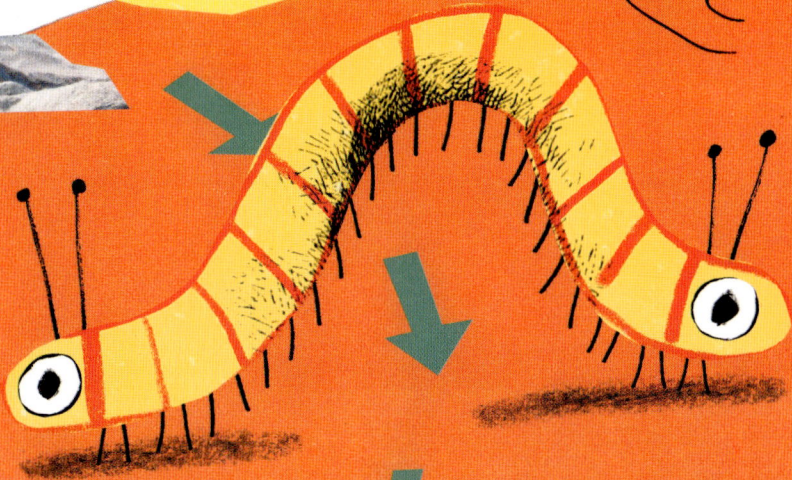

. . . until it got caught up in lots of tall, pointy things.

TEETH! Sharp teeth glinted menacingly all around them.

'These are fish. And look, down there is the deep sea,' said Lolo, who knew lots about Earth.

FANTASTIC FISH! ↗

Behold, bones! Fish were the first bony animals (known as vertebrates) in Earth's history. Today, there are 35,000 species of fish, among them are AMAZING ANGLERS, EERIE-LOOKING EELS and ELECTROSENSITIVE SHARKS!

Something had caused **CHAOS** in the **AMPHIBIAN** area.

'Hey, are these **ANIMAL FOOTPRINTS?**' Flarp asked.

The Martian friends picked their way through the displays and followed the footprints around the next corner...

HAPPY HOPPERS

Frog babies are known as tadpoles. Tadpoles swim in lakes and ponds, munching on plants. After a few weeks, they grow back legs and arms before losing their tail and crawling out of the water to live as frogs.

'Why do I feel like one of those eyes in the water isn't quite right?' asked Lolo.

'Because it's **NOT!**' shouted Flarp.

'It's the monster and it's **GETTING AWAY!**'

THE MOST UNEXPLORED HABITAT ON EARTH!

Habitats are places where animals and plants live. The biggest, by far, is the deep sea. Here, there is so little light that some animals have come up with their own ways to shine.

CORAL REEFS

Coral reefs are full of animals! More than a quarter of all ocean animals live here, including more than 4,000 types of fish.

TOOTHY TRAGEDY

Humans hunt and kill 100 million sharks each year, yet only ten humans are eaten by sharks in return. No one knows why sharks signed up to this very unfair deal.

HIGH VOLTAGE!

The electric eel can use electricity to deliver a nasty shock!

BIG FISH

This kitefin shark is the biggest luminous fish. It lights up its belly so that predators below don't see its shape.

GLOWY SHOAL

There are hundreds of different kinds of lanternfish. Each species has its own unique glowing pattern, which they use to identify one another.

ANGLERFISH

Is it a worm? A hungry fish investigates this strange glowing blob, attached to a hungry anglerfish with tooth-laden jaws.

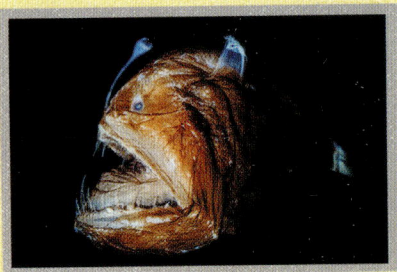

AMAZING AMPHIBIANS!

Amphibians were one of the first bony animals to conquer the Earth. Come and enjoy **TREMENDOUS TADPOLES!** Fine-tune your **FROG SONGS!** Peruse some **PECULIAR POTIONS!**

↙

TANTALISING TAILS

Male newts make special love potions for females, which they send through the water by wagging their tails back-and-forth. It smells like Martian cave dew!

FROG CHORUS

The sound of frog's mating calls can travel a mile or more. They use special pouches that blow up like ugly balloons to make the sounds.

. . . then skidded to a stop in front of the most **AMAZING CREATURES** they had ever seen.

'Dinosaurs are **AWESOME!**' said Lolo.

'We've only ever found their fossils, so no one can really be sure what they look or sound like.'

At exactly that moment a **TERRIFYING** squawk filled their ears.

'**DINOSAUR!**' they yelled, and began to run.

ROAR-SOME DINOSAURS

Long ago, huge reptiles called dinosaurs walked the Earth. We can't know for sure what they looked like, but from their bones Martian scientists think it was something like this.

REMARKABLE REPTILES!

Reptiles have leathery skin and most lay shelled eggs. They include crocodiles, lizards, snakes, turtles and their long-dead relatives, the dinosaurs. Dare to duel with their **POWERFUL JAWS**? Care to taste their **VICIOUS VENOM** or stroke their **SCALY SKIN**?

JAWS FOR THOUGHT

To stop prey from running away, crocodiles clamp their jaws shut with muscles four times stronger than those of a tiger.

POWERFUL POISON

The inland taipan's venom is so powerful that a single bite could kill 100 humans! Thankfully, Martians are immune.

'HELLO!' something squawked. 'Who's a pretty boy then?'
'What is that? What is it saying, Lolo?' asked Flarp.
'No idea,' Lolo replied.

'Is it a . . . DINOSAUR?' said Flarp.
'Hmm,' said Lolo, checking the information panel.
'Nope, JUST A BIRD. Although it says that birds
are what remain of dinosaurs. WEIRD!'

'Come on, let's go. There's no monster here,' said Flarp, impatiently.

 SQUAWK!

BETTER WITH BEAKS
Beaks can be used for
picking, plucking, squeezing
and cracking.

POPULAR PARROTS
Like humans, parrots know
lots of words. Martian
scientists are still trying to
work out whether parrots
taught humans to speak
first or if it was the other
way around.

FEATHERS

Feathers are made of keratin, the same stuff as Martian claws. By fanning them out, birds can soar and glide. By fluffing them up, they keep warm.

↖ BRILLIANT BIRDS!

With 11,000 different species of bird, the Earth sky is full of life! These feathered animals lay eggs and fly using their feathered arms. Stare in wonder at their BEWILDERING BEAKS! Examine their EXQUISITE FEATHERS!

Lolo and Flarp found themselves on the MAMMAL floor.

'Look at the size of that BLUE WHALE!' said Lolo.
'It's Earth's largest mammal,' Flarp read. 'It eats
40 million animals EACH DAY!'

Lolo gulped. 'I hope it doesn't want to EAT us too.'

'Don't be silly, Lolo. It doesn't look like it's going anywhere.'

TELLTALE TEETH

Like many animals, mammals
grow special hard bits in their
mouths called teeth. Mammal teeth
come in three shapes: incisors at the
front for nibbling, pointy canine teeth
for tugging and flat molars
at the back for chewing.

MAGNIFICENT MAMMALS!

Meet the mind-blowing mammals! Mammals are mostly hairy animals that give birth to babies without laying eggs. Explore their TERRIFYING TEETH! Listen to their STRANGE SONGS! Marvel at their MARVELLOUS MILK!

↓

BIG BLUE WHALE

This is the largest animal in the solar system. If you stacked all blue whales end to end, the distance would be ten times taller than Mars's largest volcano! Booming whale song can travel thousands of miles.

SWEATY SNACK

Mammals make a special kind of sticky sweat called milk. Milk helps baby mammals grow. Humans have been known to drink the milk of another animal – the cow!

THIS WAY TO HILARIOUS HUMANS →

Flarp noticed something ahead. 'Hey, I think there's an even SCARiER predator through here!'

'HUMANS!' cried Flarp. But he was laughing. 'I don't really think humans are scary. They are strange, though.'

'It's those WEIRD hairy eyebrows and beady eyes,' said Lolo.

'I've heard they've tried to visit Mars! But that must be rubbish – look, their brains are TOO SMALL for space travel.'

The little Martians sped on into the next hall.

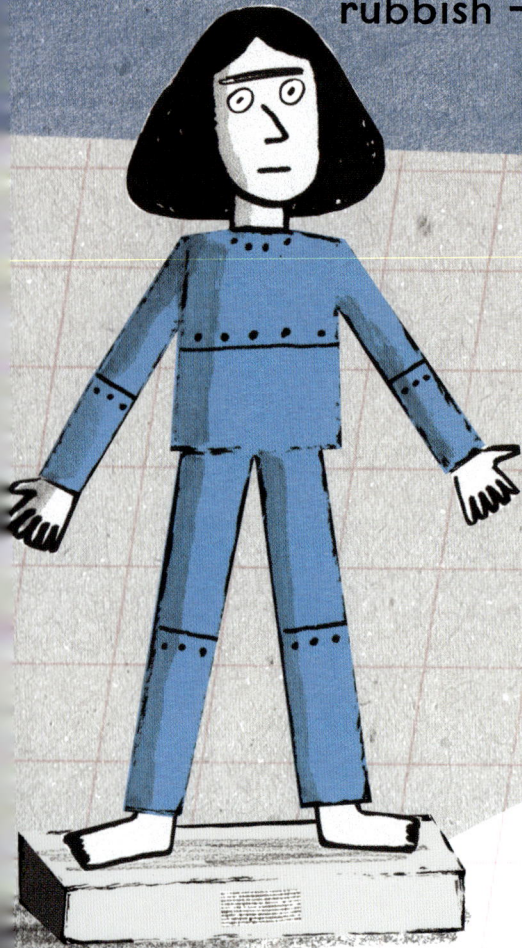

TOOLS OF THE TRADE

Like Martians, mammals are good at using tools. Chimpanzees use sticks to fish for insects. Elephants use sticks to swat buzzing insects. Humans clean their teeth using a special brush.

Beware the beady eyes! Earth animals have jelly-like eyes that can swivel around to look at things that interest them.

WE CAME IN PEACE FOR ALL MANKIND.

HILARIOUS HUMANS!

Earth is changing because of a strange ape that recently evolved there. Listen to its **CHATTERING CALLS!** Laugh at its **KNOBBLY KNEES**. Feast your eyes on its **MOVABLE THUMBS!**

MYSTERIOUS MARKINGS

Martian scientists discovered strange footprints on Earth's Moon together with this sign. We think it's probably a hoax.

Humans have lots of fingers, which can be used for nose-picking. Martians don't know how many toes they have because humans cover them with tubes (known as 'socks').

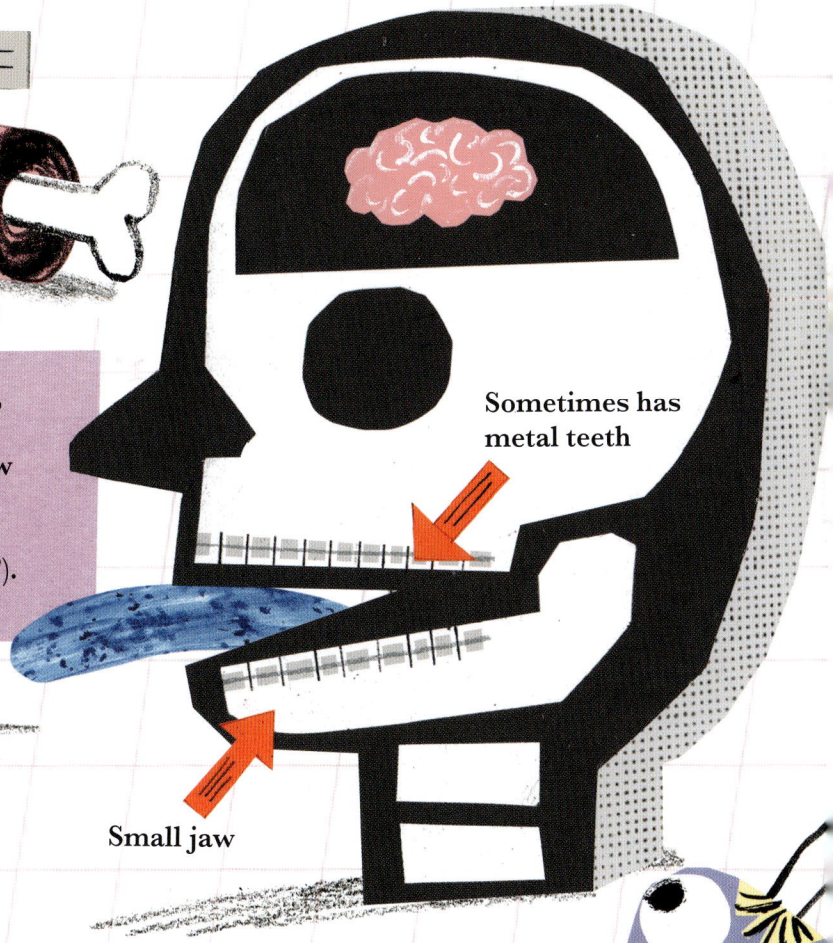

Sometimes has metal teeth

Small jaw

BUILT TO RUN!

Humans are apes with long legs. Their stilt-like limbs propel the body further, meaning that humans, a long time ago, could run across grasslands to hunt prey.

'PETS!' gasped Lolo, who had a sudden pang of missing Reeble, her fluffy little snorgle who was waiting at home. 'Listen, Flarp, it says pets can train humans to give them food and hugs!'

'Pah!' Flarp scoffed. 'Humans can't be that CLEVER if they fall for that!'

Lolo didn't say anything. Reeble liked tasty food and warm hugs too.

'No monster here!' Flarp declared.

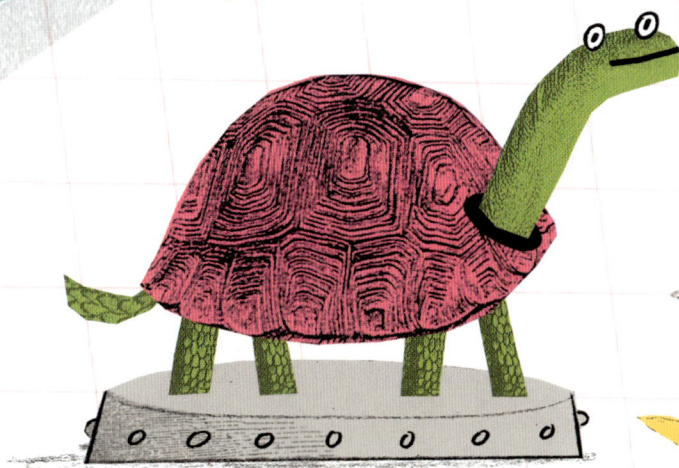

Dogs and cats train humans to cuddle and feed them! Humans even pick up their poo. Dogs can understand human words like 'sit' and 'stay' but only if there are treats around!

Many cats demand their own special entrances. For this reason, many houses have both cat flaps and human flaps (known as doors).

Cats do not demand much from their human assistants except a constant supply of food, water, soft cushions, snacks, a special post for scratching, toys, brushes, prime position in the bed and heated blankets.

Humans keep worms in giant fields. Worms keep the soil healthy.

↖ PLAYFUL PETS!

Humans have a funny habit of making friends with other animals. Here are some of their finest buddies! Which is your favourite?

The next hall was filled with the **STRANGE PLACES** where Earth animals live.

'We're **NEVER** going to catch up with the monster,' moaned Lolo.

'No,' agreed Flarp. 'Not unless . . .'

GRASSLANDS

' . . . or **slither** like a snake . . .'

'...we **glide** like a gazelle...'

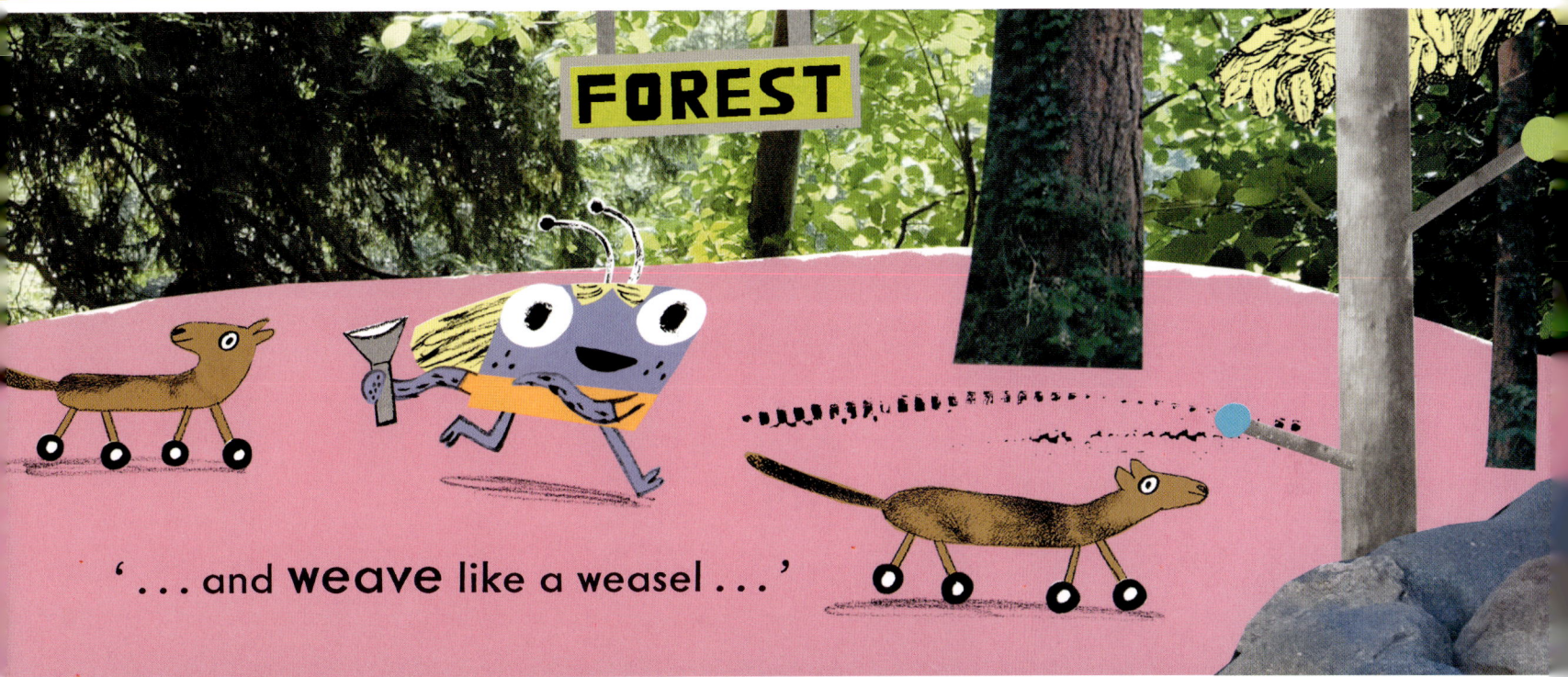

FOREST

'...and **weave** like a weasel...'

DESERT

'**WHEEEEEEE!**' called Lolo and Flarp as they raced
through vast landscapes of grass, trees and sand.

'WAIT!' said Lolo. 'What are all of these?'

Flarp peered into the gloom. 'They look like museum models that have been packed away,' he replied. 'I wonder why?'

Flarp and Lolo read the STRANGE STORIES of dodos and Tasmanian tigers and giant sea cows.

'QUICK! Over here!' said Flarp. 'I've found the MONSTER!'

'Wait, that's NOT A MONSTER!' said Lolo.
'I don't think it's even an EARTH ANIMAL!'

More than two-thirds of Earth is covered in water.

Earth has lots of cute little volcanoes.

EYE SPY EARTH! ↗

Use this telescope to see our **WATERY NEIGHBOUR**, the planet Earth for yourself! Can you spot its **ROCKY CLUMPS OF LAND**? Its white dusty **ICE CAPS**? Can you make out its **DRY DESERTS** and **LUSH GREEN FORESTS**?

There are around 3 trillion trees in the world! They help humans to breathe. That's more than 350 trees per human!

TASMANIAN TIGER

The Tasmanian Tiger belongs to a special group of mammals called marsupials. It has a pouch for its young. [EXTINCT 1936]

Then suddenly there was a loud

BANG!

STOREROOM

STAFF ONLY
BEYOND THIS
POINT

'The MONSTER!' Flarp shouted.
'That must be the monster! It's on the stairs!'

The friends scrambled upstairs as fast as they
could and arrived, panting, in the telescope room.

STOREROOM

PASSENGER PIGEON

Flocks of passenger pigeons can be so large they can block out the Sun! Numbering more than 5,000 million, this is the most common bird on Earth. Nothing can stop it! [EXTINCT 1914]

DODO

The dodo is a flightless bird that lives on an island called Mauritius. [EXTINCT 1681]

STELLER'S SEA COW

This gentle giant is more closely related to an elephant than it is to a cow. It communicates by grunting and spends most of its days eating seaweeds. [EXTINCT 1768]

Humans like to gather
in cities, which are made
up of lots of large box
shapes stacked near
each other.

The next morning, Lolo and Flarp couldn't wait to tell the rest of the class all about their adventure.

'... so that's how we met the **MARS ROVER**. We think it was trying to find its way home. Rover has wheels, an eye and makes lots of little whirring noises,' Flarp told the class.

THANK YOU FOR VISITING THE
MARTIAN MUSEUM OF EARTH ANIMALS.
WE HOPE TO SEE YOU AGAIN SOON!

MARS ROVER

'Next, we need to find out which animal made it!' said Lolo, excitedly. 'We think it was probably the BEETLES ...'

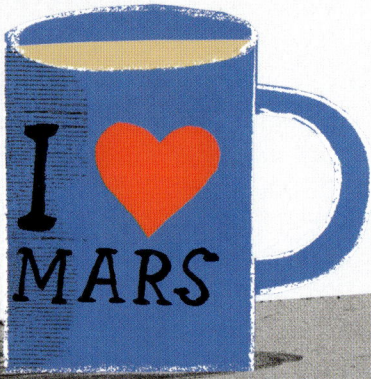

Dear Earth, are you receiving?
This is Mars Rover calling Earth.

I have been captured by Martians. Repeat.
I have been captured by Martians.

The little Martians seem very friendly and
want to know more about Earth animals.
They have expressed an interest in
travelling to Earth.

Should I confirm?

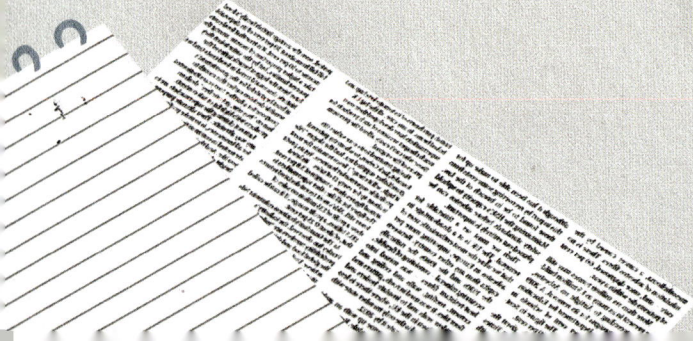

I ♥ MARS

This pen belongs to Buzz